Wisdom Is The Principle Thing
A Daily Devotional

Kimberly Moses

Copyright © 2019 by Kimberly Moses

All rights reserved. No part of this publication may be reproduced by any means, graphics, electronic, or mechanical, including photocopying, recording, taping, or by any information storage retrieval system without the written permission of the publisher except in the case of brief quotations embodied in critical articles and reviews.

Kimberly Moses/Rejoice Essential Publishing
PO BOX 512
Effingham, SC 29541

www.republishing.org

Unless otherwise indicated, scripture is taken from the King James Version.

Wisdom Is The Principle Thing/ Kimberly Moses

ISBN-10: 1-946756-46-6
ISBN-13: 978-1-946756-46-6
Library of Congress Control Number:2018915290

DEDICATION

I dedicate this book to everyone that supports my ministry and to all my students; past, current, and future. Thank you Tron Moses for supporting me and being my biggest support system.

Table of Contents

ACKNOWLEDGMENTS......................................xi

What Is Wisdom..1

Benefits Of Wisdom..6

Prayers For Wisdom...18

Devotion One..22

Devotion Two...25

Devotion Three..28

Devotion Four..31

Devotion Five...34

Devotion Six...37

Devotion Seven..40

Devotion Eight...43

Devotion Nine..46

Devotion Ten...49

Devotion Eleven...52

Devotion Twelve..55

Devotion Thirteen..58

Devotion Fourteen...61

Devotion Fifteen..64

Devotion Sixteen..67

Devotion Seventeen...70

Devotion Eighteen..73

Devotion Nineteen...76

Devotion Twenty..79

Devotion Twenty One..82

Devotion Twenty Two..85

Devotion Twenty Three.......................................88

Devotion Twenty Four...91

Devotion Twenty Five..94

Devotion Twenty Six..97

Devotion Twenty Seven.....................................100

Devotion Twenty Eight......................................103

Devotion Twenty Nine.......................................106

Devotion Thirty..109

Devotion Thirty One..112

Devotion Thirty Two..115

Devotion Thirty Three.......................................118

Devotion Thirty Four..121

Devotion Thirty Five...124

Devotion Thirty Six...127

Devotion Thirty Seven..130

Devotion Thirty Eight...133

Devotion Thirty Nine..136

Devotion Forty..139

Devotion Forty One..142

Devotion Forty Two..145

Devotion Forty Three...148

Devotion Forty Four...151

Devotion Forty Five..154

Devotion Forty Six..157

Devotion Forty Seven...160

Devotion Forty Eight..163

Devotion Forty Nine...166

ABOUT THE AUTHOR....................................169

REFERENCE..178

ACKNOWLEDGMENTS

This book wouldn't be possible without the inspiration of the Holy Spirit. He gave me the blueprint and I just obeyed as I wrote the manuscript.

2 Timothy 3:16-17 says, "All scripture is given by inspiration of God, and is profitable for doctrine, for reproof, for correction, for instruction in righteousness: That the man of God may be perfect, thoroughly furnished unto all good works."

What Is Wisdom?

Every day we must make decisions. We decide what to eat. For instance, are you going to eat a bowl of cereal, a bagel, or pancakes, etc. for breakfast? We decide what to wear. Are you going to wear short sleeves, a tank top, or a sweater? We decide if we want to have good hygiene or not. Do we brush our teeth every day, every other day, or three times a day, etc? Do we skip taking a shower or bath today? Do we wear deodorant or not? We must decide spiritual things. We decide if we are going to go to church, read the bible, or pray? What religion will we be a part of? We decide who we date or marry. The point is that every day we make numerous amounts of choices.

Therefore wisdom is needed. Wisdom will guide us in the decisions we make. According to Merriam Webster, wisdom can be defined as the ability to discern inner qualities and relationships: INSIGHT, good sense: JUDGMENT.[1] Without wisdom, we will get connected to the wrong people and live a destructive lifestyle. Without wisdom, we will break laws and be a menace to society. Without wisdom, we can't judge the difference between good and evil. In other words, without wisdom, we will lack common sense.

God loves to give us wisdom because it's a gift (James 1:5). He loves us so much that He wants us to make the right choices and with His wisdom; we are able to make the best decisions. Many people make decisions and don't consider the consequences. However, when we walk in wisdom, we will consider the pros and the cons before we even decide. God wants His children to be blessed, prosperous, and healthy. If we lack wisdom, then it's a huge possibility that we won't be blessed, prosperous, or healthy because we allowed the devil to come in with bad decision making such as having spent all our money when we should've been saving it, getting in toxic relationships, having unprotected sex outside of marriage and getting STDs, drinking alcohol to the point where liver diseases develops, and the list continues.

I have made a lot of mistakes in my life. I have been in the wrong relationships which caused me harm and resulted in me losing everything. I have tried drugs which could've killed me if I got addicted. I lived a fast life which resulted in guns being pulled on me, community service, stress, depression, and so on. I have acted out in anger which resulted in me doing probation for two years. I can write several books, which I had done already on my stupidity. I didn't start to even consider my decision making until I went through a wilderness season. In this season, I encountered God in a new way.

I was faced with jail time and probation. There was no way out of it. I had to serve and do time. All my life, I got out of doing things because I could manipulate my way out of something. But this time, I wasn't in control. In these dark moments, is when I discovered how real the Lord truly is. I had to grow up; I broke down and cried out to God. I had truly repented. My eyes began to open. I could see my stupidity. I saw how angry and bitter I'd become. I realized that my lifestyle was destructive. God gave me wisdom when I asked for His help. I found that I had the strength to say NO to bad choices. I found that I had the strength to walk away from SIN. I found that I could thoroughly map out all the consequences to a decision before acting out on it rashly.

God began to strip me of the junk in my heart. He got rid of the pride, lust, selfishness, hatred, anger, perversion, pettiness, fear, and the list goes on. He began to isolate me by disconnecting me from the wrong people. He began to speak to me and convict me, so I knew the difference from right and wrong. My life was no longer mines. The Lord had His hands upon me. Over time, my mind began to change because I was thinking differently. I knew that if I opened certain doors than the consequences would cost me everything. I asked God for wisdom, and He gave me an abundance of it. He will do the same for you.

We will cover a lot of vital principles throughout this book. There are 49 devotions that consist of a daily scripture to meditate on. Meditation will get the word deep within your heart. Once the word gets deep within your heart, it will begin to take root. Once it takes root, it will grow and eventually bear fruit. Also, the devotions consist of a further expounding of the word that will cause a significant change in your life. Lastly, I give a little of my testimony or life experiences that will encourage you to apply the wisdom of God in your life. Get ready to grow in this gift called wisdom. Remember, wisdom is the principle thing.

Benefits Of Wisdom

There are twelve benefits to this gift of wisdom. Whenever we live God's way, then we reap blessings. We will closely explore each of these benefits.

1. Protection

Whenever we obey God, He will protect us in this evil wicked world. No matter what plots the devil has for us, it won't work when we have

God's protection. For instance, the enemy could be planning a plane crash to kill you and your assignment, but God will warn you. We win every time, and the devil fails all the time. So how does wisdom cause God's protection? Easy. Look at Proverbs 3:25-26.

"Be not afraid of sudden fear, neither of the desolation of the wicked, when it cometh. For the Lord shall be thy confidence and shall keep thy foot from being taken."

When you obey God's instruction that is a very wise thing to do. As a result of your decision to obey Him, then you don't have to be afraid of terror. When everyone around you is in panic mode, you will have peace because deep down you will know that God will protect you, your family, and your belongings. You can have confidence in Him because you know that if He did it before then He can do it again. You can know that Your feet won't stumble in the devil's trap because God always provides a way of escape.

2. Guidance

Have you ever been in a situation and didn't know what to do? This is where wisdom comes in. Wisdom is the "How to" do something in any circumstance. Apostle Ryan Lestrange stated that "Word of Wisdom is the How to." When I heard him say that, I immediately received clarity on this spiritual gift.

1 Corinthians 12:8 says, "For to one is given by the Spirit the word of wisdom; to another the word of knowledge by the same Spirit;"

Many times, I knew what God wanted to do, but I didn't know how He wanted to do it. I knew what God wanted me to do, but I didn't always know how. This is how wisdom provides guidance. When you look at Proverbs 3:6, you can clearly see that God will direct your paths when you acknowledge Him and listen to Him.

Proverbs 3:6 says, "In all thy ways acknowledge him, and he shall direct thy paths."

3. Long life

When we obey God, we are spared from destruction and unnecessary heartache. As a result, we will have a promise of a long life. We won't make bad choices that could end our lives such as overdosing on drugs because wisdom will tell us to not even do drugs.

Proverbs 3: 16 says, "Length of days is in her right hand; and in her left-hand riches and honour."

As we look at the verse above, we can see wisdom offers the length of days which means long life. Wisdom gives you the ability to avoid foolish choices that could cost you your life.

4. Good health

When we apply God's wisdom, we make better choices overall. This includes resisting the devil and praying more to not be led into temptation. You can resist the urge to avoid choices that cause sickness in your body. Many people are sick because they don't exercise and make the wrong choices when eating food. They eat high-calorie foods that are full of sugar and fat. Eventually, they get diabetes, heart disease, and a host of other ailments that are tied to their diet. Wisdom will cause us to take care of our bodies.

Proverbs 4:22 says, "For they are life unto those that find them, and health to all their flesh."

5. Happiness

When we apply God's word to our lives, we have a sense of contentment. We can be happy because the void in our hearts will be filled with God and His love. We know that He is pleased with us because we are in right standing with Him. This is a level of freedom that wisdom brings us. We can be happy and free from things that once had us bound.

Proverbs 3:13 says, "Happy is the man that findeth wisdom, and the man that getteth understanding."

6. Riches and honor

God wants us to succeed in life. He wants us to prosper and to teach us how to profit (Isaiah 48:17). He delights in our prosperity (Psalms 35:27). When we listen to Him, He can give us ideas and the resources for success. He can give us dreams, visions, etc. that will show us how to generate an abundance of income. He will favor us and cause wealth in our lives. God will even cause people to honor you when you are wise. Many people will come and seek after you like they did King Solomon because of his wisdom.

Proverbs 3: 16 says, "Length of days is in her right hand; and in her left-hand riches and honour."

Proverbs 3:35 says, "The wise shall inherit glory (honor): but shame shall be the promotion of fools."

7. Peace

When we have wisdom, we can have peace knowing that we have made the best decision.

There is nothing worse than feeling condemned about something you've done in your past or regretting the dumb choices you made. Wisdom will lift those heavy burdens we carry and give our spirits a sense of ease because we can know that we are in the will of God and that He is pleased. We can have freedom in our minds because the devil has no legal right to torment us because we made the best choice in the sight of God. Peace is a byproduct of wisdom, and it belongs to us as children of God.

Proverbs 3:17 says, "Her ways are ways of pleasantness, and all her paths are peace."

James 3:17 says, "But the wisdom that is from above is first pure, then peaceable, gentle, and easy to be intreated, full of mercy and good fruits, without partiality, and without hypocrisy."

8. Stumble free walk

Every day we must walk circumspectly because the devil is trying to tempt us with sinful things that our flesh loves. He tries to get us off the right path in life and turn our backs on God by baiting us with fame, riches, and other things that are lustful to our eyes. When we walk in wisdom, we won't allow our flesh to lead us. We will allow the Spirit of God to lead us. We will get supernatural power to resist the enemy and watch out for his traps. The Holy Spirit will warn us by giving us checks in our spirit that something isn't right about people or different circumstances. Maybe we will have dreams about something that is a warning from God, so we don't stumble. Perhaps, God will send a prophet, or someone to expose the enemy's plans. Wisdom will bless us to be stumble free in this journey.

Proverbs 3:23 says, "Then shalt thou walk in thy way safely, and thy foot shall not stumble."

9. Anxiety free

I had anxiety for five years. Anxiety was a result of the bad choices I made. I committed sexual sins and backslid. When this happened, a portal to hell opened in my life and the devil wasn't going anywhere until I made a decision to get back on the right track. Every day for five years, I heard the devil telling me that I was going to die, I was sick, and that he was going to kill me. I was afraid to leave my house and when I did leave my home, I had panic attacks. It was truly hard to function in life. When I repented and started living right, God delivered me. Deliverance from anxiety was a long process, for up to five years. Sin is not worth losing your peace. I truly suffered from making bad choices.

Proverbs 3:25 Be not afraid of sudden fear, neither of the desolation of the wicked, when it cometh.

10. Sweet sleep

As you can see wisdom will protect you from the enemy. One of the schemes of the enemy is to attack us in our sleep. He looks for various ways to attack us. When we are asleep, we are vulnerable. We aren't up praying, fasting, or reading our bibles. We are quiet and still. Who is watching over us when we are asleep? God (Psalms 121:4; 127:2). When we aren't in His will, then the enemy can legally torment us. Sometimes the devil attacks us in our dreams because we are ignorant of the word of God, have a weak prayer life, or from backlash. Whatever the case is, when we walk in wisdom by making the best choices, God will give us sweet sleep. I wish I knew this a long time ago because demons tormented me in the night for years. Some of them were sexual and tried to kiss and caress me. Some of them tried to smother me and possess me. Now, since I am knowledgeable of demonic attacks and the promise of sweet sleep, the devil doesn't torment me in the night anymore.

Proverbs 3:24 says, "When thou liest down, thou shalt not be afraid: yea, thou shalt lie down, and thy sleep shall be sweet."

11. Promotion

When we walk uprightly and obey the commandments of the Lord, then there are benefits. This is a very wise thing to do and will cause God to supernaturally promote you. Have you ever been frustrated because you tried to market or promote yourself or brand, but it wasn't working? I have learned that it is better for God to promote you because when He does it, then it's effortless. There is no frustration when God promotes you, the doors just swing wide open. For a season, I tried to promote my books, videos, and ministry. I was so discouraged because no one was interested. I was overlooked. When I shifted my focus and made the right choices on how I would invest my time, then God promoted me. He caused an increase in my book sells, more views on my videos, an increase of likes on social media, and divine connections in ministry. Making the right choices will result in a promotion from God.

Proverbs 4:8 says, "Exalt her, and she shall promote thee: she shall bring thee to honour, when thou dost embrace her."

12. Confidence

When you walk in wisdom and obey everything that the Lord tells you to do, then you will have heaven's backing. You can be confident in God that if He said it, then He will back you up. If God sent you, then He will show up in a powerful way. God won't leave you high and dry. He has you. When God told me to do a conference, I was afraid at first, but I quickly realize that if He wanted me to do it, then He would provide the finances. That's exactly what He did. I put my confidence in Him and He came through. I had confidence that the sick would be healed at the conference and miracles would happen. God gave me wisdom and everything that I labored for manifested.

Proverbs 3:26 says, "For the Lord shall be thy confidence, and shall keep thy foot from being taken."

Now that we have explored these benefits, we will move on to prayer. These aren't all the benefits of wisdom. As you read the book of Proverbs, your eyes will open, and you can see some benefits. Also, as you read each devotion further along in this book, you will also see other benefits that will shift your life.

Prayers

Lord, bless me with wisdom in Jesus name.

I decree that I will be wise and fear the Lord and depart from evil (Job 28:28).

I decree that I will offer godly counsel that is good. I will teach right from wrong (Psalm 37:30).

I decree that I will heed the warnings from the Lord and consider His great love (Psalm 107:43).

I decree that I will fear the Lord because it is the beginning of all wisdom. I will follow His precepts and have a great understanding (Psalm 111:10).

I decree that the fear of the Lord is the foundation of true knowledge. I will not be foolish and despise the Lord's wisdom and discipline (Proverbs 1:7).

I will not be wise in my own eyes, but I will fear the Lord and turn away from evil (Proverbs 3:7).

Wisdom is the principal thing. In all my getting, I decree that I will get understanding (Proverbs 4:7).

I decree that wisdom will be found on my lips (Proverbs 10:13).

I decree that I will be watchful with my lips and refrain from speaking when it's unnecessary (Proverbs 10:19).

I decree that I will be humble because it comes with wisdom (Proverbs 11:2).

I decree that I will be a soul winner because he who wins souls is wise (Proverbs 11:30).

I decree that my words will bring healing to others because the tongue of the wise brings healing (Proverbs 12:18).

I decree that I will remain teachable and listen to those in authority.

I decree that I will be open to take advice and instruction from those who you place in my life.

I decree that I will avoid foolish conversations.

I decree that I will build my house and not tear it

down (Proverbs 14:1).

I decree that I will be diligent and discerning in Jesus name.

I decree that I will make wise choices and not grieve the spirit of God.

I decree that I will stay on the straight and narrow path in Jesus name.

I decree that I will control my temper and walk in forgiveness.

I decree that I will meditate on your word and get your word deep within my heart.

I decree that I will be disciplined and led by your spirit.

I decree that I will let my light shine, so you can get the glory out of my life.

I decree that I will shun evil and walk uprightly in Jesus name.

I decree that I will pray about everything and everyone in the name of Jesus.

I decree that the Lord will order my steps.

Lord, bless me with the gift of the word of wisdom and increase that anointing on my life.

Bless me to be a good steward of my finances.

Bless my heart to be pleasing in your sight.

Bless me to think the right thoughts.

I rebuke having a carnal mind in Jesus name.

Lord, give me the spirit of wisdom so I can impart it into the lives of others in Jesus name.

Bless me to get to know you more and reveal the mysteries of your kingdom.

DEVOTION ONE

Today's Scripture For Meditation

Job 12:13 says, "With him is wisdom and strength, he hath counsel and understanding."

There is a lot of advice that we can find in today's society. We can look up a certain topic with a click of a button on the internet. We can ask our smart devices to look up something for us. Finding information is becoming easier than ever. This is great; however, we must take heed and check the source of the information. Is it credible? If we aren't careful, then we could be deceived into believing something that's not true. God's wisdom proves to be true and the best source. He is waiting for us to cry out and ask Him for wisdom. When we do this, we won't be deceived by other sources.

People will give you all sorts of counsel. Some counsel might be great and in the will of God for your life while some counsel is straight up carnal and will grieve the spirit of God. God's spirit will never lead us astray and it's up to us to apply the tools and the instructions that He has given us. Many times, I had to fall on my face in deep prayer and ask God for a strategy. When I did, God gave me counsel and a greater depth of understanding. Remember, in God is your true source of wisdom, revelation, understanding, and all things.

Dear Heavenly Father,

I humble myself today. I repent for not always seeking your counsel and doing things on my own. Bless me Lord to be a person of prayer. Lord, I truly want to seek your face and take heed to your counsel. I don't want to be deceived by the schemes of the enemy. Lord, open my spiritual eyes so I will be able to discern both good and evil. Lord, remove any ungodly influences out of my life, so I don't go down the wrong path in life. I pray that I will come to you first and ask you before I ask anyone else for advice. Thank you for answering this prayer in Jesus' name. Amen.

DEVOTION TWO

Today's Scripture For Meditation

Psalm 90:12 says, "So teach us to number our days, that we may apply our hearts unto wisdom."

Life is truly short. One day we are here and the next day we are in eternity. It seems like the years fly by and we have memories of our childhood and pivotal moments embedded in our hearts. Don't waste your life and not apply yourself. What will your legacy be? What will people say about you when you leave this earth? Have you obeyed everything the Lord told you to do? Have you pursued that dream of something major that you want to do in the back of your mind? We need to live life with a purpose.

A purposeful life is an impactful life. People are impacted by you as you walk in purpose. God will give us the wisdom to walk effectively in purpose. He will order our steps and guide us along the way, so we know what to do in the small and big things in life. My biggest desire is that I fulfill my assignment and do everything the Lord placed on my heart to do before God calls me home. I live a purposeful life and you can too. God wants us to carry His word in our hearts and apply it to our lives because we have work to do.

Dear Heavenly Father,

I humble myself. I repent for the times I procrastinated and didn't obey what you told me to do. Forgive me, Lord. I realize that one day, we all will die. I want my life to be one of purpose. Lord, bless me to fulfill my assignment in this earth and make me aware of my purpose as never before. Lord, I don't want to waste any more time, but I decree that I will live a life of productivity. I come against stagnancy and slothfulness in Jesus' name. Amen.

DEVOTION THREE

Today's Scripture For Meditation

Proverbs 1:5 says, "A wise man will hear, and will increase learning; and a man of understanding shall attain unto wise counsels:"

God has placed certain people in our lives that are seasoned or have more life experiences than us. We must remain teachable and listen to their counsel. Many times, we might not want to hear the counsel of our leaders or those that we might be submitted to, but if we obey what they instructed us, then we will be spared experiencing destruction. If we know that the people in our lives have the heart of God for us, then we should be able to trust that they will counsel us in the will of God.

I am thankful for the leaders in my life. They can give me insight on things that I might not see or warn me because they have walked the path where I am walking. I must be mindful to pray to God and seek Him after I receive counsel from my leaders. When I submit to leadership, then a greater level of wisdom comes to my life as well as a greater anointing. I must study the word of God to make sure my leaders are telling me things that are in the will of God for my life. I realize that when my leadership critiques me, it's an opportunity to grow. Remember, no one knows everything. Remain humble and have people around you that aren't afraid to tell you the truth about yourself even if it hurts.

Dear Heavenly Father,

I am truly grateful that you placed godly people in my life to give me sound advice. Lord, bless me to have the right spirit where I can receive advice and not take offense. Lord, show me the hearts of these people so that I know that they are coming from a place of love. I bind up any attacks of my mind where pride, deception, and hardness of heart can enter in. Lord, even if I don't agree with everything bless me to come to you with all things in prayer and allow me to be meek. Thank you for answering this prayer in Jesus' name. Amen.

DEVOTION FOUR

Today's Scripture For Meditation

Proverbs 1:7 says, "The fear of the LORD is the beginning of knowledge: but fools despise wisdom and instruction."

When we become aware of who God truly is, we don't want to grieve His Holy Spirit. We will gain a level of reverence for Him that we didn't have before. We come to the full realization that He is the ultimate source of everything. It all starts with Him. He is the creator of the universe and mankind. There is nothing new under the sun. When you have the fear of the Lord, then you won't make devastating mistakes that will cost you your life or anointing.

Foolish people feel like no one can tell them anything. They are hard to deal with. They reject counsel and oftentimes they fall hard on their faces. I have seen leaders fall straight on their faces. They started off pure but along the way they became tainted with sin and they stopped fearing God. God warned them plenty of times to repent and extended His mercy. It wasn't until public exposure or humiliation they were humbled. In the humbling process, they remembered that God was the beginning of knowledge.

Dear Heavenly Father,

Lord, allow me to always look to you and not take my eyes off your son Jesus. Sometimes distractions happen in life that will cause me to lose focus, but I want to be mindful that when I reverence you and respect you, that is the first step to wisdom. Lord, guard my heart against pride, greed, lust, carnality and anything else that will lead me astray. Give me wisdom so I can make better choices in life. Thank you, for answering this prayer in Jesus' name. Amen.

DEVOTION FIVE

Today's Scriptures For Meditation

Proverbs 2:6-7 says, "For the Lord giveth wisdom: out of his mouth cometh knowledge and understanding. He layeth up sound wisdom for the righteous: he is a buckler to them that walk uprightly."

God wants His children to receive everything that they can from Him. Part of that everything includes wisdom. God knows everything and will never lead us astray because He is the spirit of truth. He knows what doors we should walk through and what doors we should avoid. When He speaks a word, we should listen and obey. Once we yield to Him, He will pour out an extra measure of wisdom called "sound wisdom." This wisdom is supernatural and causes breakthrough, provision, protection, and insight in many areas. You might not understand why God may prevent you from doing certain things, but it's for your protection because He is your buckler.

For years, I wanted to launch a mentorship program, but the timing was never right. I got remarried. I had a couple of preaching engagements. I had an ordination service. I was a vendor at several conferences. All these things were in addition to me being a mother, wife, spiritual mother, publisher, and an author. When I felt the time was right, God said, "Wait!" Then He explained why. Sometimes, we have great ideas, but it's just not the right season. When it's the right timing, God will pour out His blessings upon it and give you the wisdom to walk in the season. Wisdom will cause you to wait for the timing of the Lord.

Dear Heavenly Father,

I thank you for giving me instructions for my life. I pray that I will always obey them. Lord, bless me to be in your timing. Many times, I may have a great idea, but I want to make sure that you approve of it and that I am in your will. Lord, bless me with sound wisdom so I can know what to do in every situation. Thank you, Lord, for giving me prophetic insight about things. I pray that you bless my heart with knowledge and understanding, in Jesus' name. Amen.

DEVOTION SIX

Today's Scriptures For Meditation

Proverbs 3:13-18 says, "Happy is the man that findeth wisdom, and the man that getteth understanding. For the merchandise of it is better than the merchandise of silver, and the gain thereof than fine gold. She is more precious than rubies: and all the things thou canst desire are not to be compared unto her. Length of days is in her right hand; and in her left-hand riches and honour. Her ways are ways of pleasantness, and all her paths are peace. She is a tree of life to them that lay hold upon her: and happy is every one that retaineth her."

Wisdom is so valuable. The scriptures tell us to not only get wisdom but to get an understanding. We are blessed when we obtain wisdom. It's more valuable silver, gold, rubies, and nothing can be compared to it. Whenever you obtain wisdom, you get access to certain promises such as long life, riches, and honor. Wisdom is something that is desirable and will bring great peace to our lives. Wisdom will make you stronger because you will learn from your experiences.

As each year goes by, I learn how to improve and how to make the conferences, classes, publishing, and any tasks that God has destined for me to do, better. I learned that as new situations arise, then I can seek God for His counsel and He will direct my paths. Over time, some reoccurring situations arose, and I was already prepared and equipped to handle it. I prayed for God to give me wisdom, so I can make the best decisions and it works every time. When you encounter a greater level of wisdom, you will encounter a greater level of blessings.

Dear Heavenly Father,

I thank you for bestowing upon me wisdom when I ask. I realize how truly valuable wisdom is and I am glad to seek you for it. I just don't want only wisdom, but I truly want to get a deeper understanding of it. Lord, give me revelation and increase my discernment of your word. Show me which paths to take and always order my steps. Allow me to reap the promises in today's passage which is long life, riches, honor, pleasantness, and peace. Thank you, for answering this prayer in Jesus name. Amen.

DEVOTION SEVEN

Today's Scriptures For Meditation

Proverbs 4:5-9 says, "Get wisdom, get understanding: forget it not; neither decline from the words of my mouth. Forsake her not, and she shall preserve thee: love her, and she shall keep thee. Wisdom is the principal thing; therefore get wisdom: and with all thy getting get understanding.

Exalt her, and she shall promote thee: she shall bring thee to honour, when thou dost embrace her. She shall give to thine head an ornament of grace: a crown of glory shall she deliver to thee."

God warns us constantly in various scriptures to not forsake His word, commands, and His ways. When we pay close attention, we can see that wisdom can spare our lives from the attacks of the enemy. Wisdom will help us discern demonic attacks and help us decline an invitation to sin, not to get off the right path, and not to be in the wrong place at the wrong time. If we truly apply the word of God to our lives then over time, we will see the hand of the Lord bring promotion and increase to us.

Have you ever heard someone say, "I should have listened to so and so?" This is how wisdom is. We must take heed to its warnings. When I was younger, I was a rebellious kid. My mother warned me to not hang out with certain girls, but I didn't listen. She just knew that they were troublemakers and could discern pass their outward shell right into their motives. One day, these group of girls and me decided to kick down someone's front door. I didn't kick it down, but I was guilty by association, and we all got in trouble. God places wise counsel in our lives for a reason. One of those reasons is to prevent us from going down the path of destruction.

Dear Heavenly Father,

I repent of any rebellion that I may have in my heart. I don't want to be in the wrong place at the wrong time. I don't want to enter on the broad pathway of destruction. I don't want to feel Hell's fire. Help me listen to wise counsel in my life because you place these people here to help me stay in your will. I decree that I will not forsake your word but will honor your ways. Thank you, for answering this prayer in Jesus name. Amen.

DEVOTION EIGHT

Today's Scripture For Meditation

Proverbs 10:8 says, "The wise in heart will receive commandments: but a prating fool shall fall."

Some of the wisest people are the people that don't say much. They don't want to draw excess attention, and they know how to walk away from drama and dismiss foolish conversations. A foolish person, on the other hand, will blurt out everything that comes to mind. There is no filter. Sometimes it's better to think before you speak. Also, it's better to process the situation before you react. A wise person will gladly welcome any advice from their leaders or those who watch over their souls. A fool will reject counsel and dismiss it.

Many years ago, I worked in the hospital around a foolish girl. She would blurt out everything that came to her mind, and most comments were offensive. She failed to listen to the supervisor multiple times. She eventually got fired. It took a lot of prayers for me to work in that hostile environment, but God kept me strong. I was able to hold my peace and didn't allow the young girl's comments to get me out of character. Continue to do the right thing no matter how challenging the situation may be.

Dear Heavenly Father,

Lord, bless me to always take heed to your warnings. Bless me to be teachable, receive instructions, and bring glory to you. I don't want to be a talkative fool. I don't know everything. I realize that I am always learning new things and there is plenty of room for me to grow and improve. Lord, bless me to stay humble and not get into my flesh. Thank you, in Jesus' name. Amen.

DEVOTION NINE

Today's Scripture For Meditation

Proverbs 10:23 says, "It is as sport to a fool to do mischief: but a man of understanding hath wisdom."

Have you ever seen someone who is always in trouble or they are very destructive in nature?

This is someone who lives on the edge and breaks all the laws and rules set in place. This person thrives on the thrill of a near-death experience, almost getting caught, and racing against the clock. Doing mischief is what they do best, and it's a sport. Everything is a game to them. Don't take pleasure in doing mischief but be a person of wisdom and great understanding.

One of my cousins spent most of his adult life doing mischief. He would rent cars and wouldn't return them. He would ditch the rental in another state somewhere and burn it. He would scam women out of their money. He would pretend that he liked them, and they would spend all their money on him. He would ditch them and move to the next women who would fall for his lies. He would destroy property, write fraudulent checks, and steal people's identity. He probably committed every imaginable crime underneath the sun. One day, he got very sick and checked into a hospital. The priest came and prayed with him because the doctors told our family that he was about to die. In that very critical moment, he repented of all his sins and accepted Jesus as his Lord and Savior. A few days afterwards, he was miraculously healed. He is now on the right track in life. My cousin was blessed because God intervened in his life at a crucial time. However, you might not be, so make each day count and live a life that is pleasing to God.

Dear Heavenly Father,

I repent of any mischief in my heart. I realize that your word tells me how wicked the heart truly is (Jeremiah 17:9). I decree that I am a person whose heart is wise and in all my getting, I will get understanding. I decree that I will pause and pray to you before I make any decision whether small or big. I refuse to allow Satan to use me. Lord, always order my steps in Jesus' name. Amen.

DEVOTION TEN

Today's Scripture For Meditation

Proverbs 11:2 says, "When pride cometh, then cometh shame: but with the lowly is wisdom."

Why does shame follow pride? The answer is because pride comes before destruction. Whenever you are on top and have everything that you may desire, if you lose all of that then it could be very shameful. People that are watching your life will see how you have hit rock bottom. King Nebuchadnezzar was a very prideful King. God sent His prophet Daniel to warn him several times to repent and to humble himself. He failed to listen, and he ate grass in the field like an ox (Daniel 4:33). That's very shameful because he lost his mind and people were watching. God blessed him to get his kingdom back after he confessed that all Glory belongs to God.

Whenever you are humble, you have a level of wisdom that a prideful person doesn't. To be honest, no one knows everything. They may be good at something, but there is so much room to grow and to approve. An old friend of mines had a supervisor that was very prideful. He didn't receive any constructive criticism that would improve the overall workplace. This supervisor came down with an iron fist and was full of arrogance. He was eventually demoted from that position and had the same title and position as everyone else. His heart was full of shame. Remain teachable because it will take you far in life.

Dear Heavenly Father,

I exalt you. I repent of my sins. Please get any pride out of my heart. Bless me to stay humble and be a person who is full of your wisdom. I don't want to get big-headed and feel like I know everything. I always want to depend on you. Lord, I truly need you, and I want to take you with me everywhere I go. Thank you, for answering this prayer in Jesus' name. Amen.

DEVOTION ELEVEN

Today's Scripture For Meditation

Proverbs 12:15 says, "The way of a fool is right in his own eyes: but he that hearkeneth unto counsel is wise."

When multiple people tell you the same thing repeatedly, then it's best to take heed. People can sometimes see better when they are looking from the outside in. For instance, a spiritual leader with no attachment can see all the red flags. When we hearken unto counsel, then we are wise because we won't have to experience heartache, failure, loss, etc. that the people who are counseling us are providing. A foolish person can't see past their own motives and agenda.

One day, a man who felt like he knew everything failed to take heed to his wife's counsel. She would try to help by making various suggestions. Her heart's motives weren't to lead the marriage but to be her husband's helpmeet. However, her husband saw it as her trying to control the marriage. The wife became frustrated and marital strife began to occur. The wife did all she knew to do which was to pray. God convicted her husband and one day as he was scrolling on Facebook, he saw a status. The status truly picked his heart. It was about husbands allowing their wives to help them and receive their counsel. After he read that status, he repented and went to his wife and apologized. She was very glad, and their marriage was restored. Remember to hearken unto wise counsel and you won't go astray.

Dear Heavenly Father,

I repent of my sins. Forgive me for the times I rejected wise counsel and found out the hard way by falling on my face. Help me to learn from my mistakes and move forward in life. I humble myself, and I decree that I will take heed to the wise, godly counsel of the voices that you placed in my life. Lord, change my perspective on how I see things to the way you see things. Bless me to come into the knowledge of you in Jesus' name. Amen.

DEVOTION TWELVE

Today's Scripture For Meditation

Proverbs 13:10 says, "Only by pride cometh contention: but with the well advised is wisdom."

A prideful person is a very argumentative person. They will cut you off in the middle of you speaking. They will over talk you and always feel like they need to interject. They are rude and belittling of others. Contention follows them. However, a wise person will take advice even if they don't fully agree with everything. They will keep the good advice and disregard the bad advice. God will give a wise person the supernatural ability to discern what's in His will for their lives.

Years ago, there was an apostle who allowed pride and bitterness to enter his heart. He was hurt by someone who attended his congregation. His whole sermons were full of contention, and he preached against the person who hurt him. The congregation knew who the apostle was talking about and they even turned on this individual. However, I was the only friend of the person that everyone else was against. God had me give a harsh word to the apostle, but he didn't take heed. A week went by and another preacher humiliated this apostle in front of his congregation by giving a corrective prophecy.

Immediately, the apostle humbled himself and apologized to the individual that hurt him and to everyone else. He realized that he was causing his church to operate in hatred instead of the love of

God. Remember that a wise person takes advice. You don't want God to expose you publicly because you fail to repent privately.

Dear Heavenly Father,

I bless anyone that has ever hurt me, and I forgive them. I decree that I refuse to be bitter and full of hatred. Lord, place a special love in my heart so I can be able to pray for those that despitefully use me and persecute me. Bless me to yield to godly counsel and stay in your will always. Thank you so much for answering this prayer in Jesus' name. Amen.

DEVOTION THIRTEEN

Today's Scripture For Meditation

Proverbs 13:20 says, "He that walketh with wise men shall be wise: but a companion of fools shall be destroyed."

When you spend time with people, you will notice that you began to pick up certain habits.

Wisdom Is The Principle Thing

For instance, you may start to repeat something you heard someone in your circle say. You may begin to flow like how they flow when they minister. Iron will sharpen iron. However, the scripture says that a companion of fools will be destroyed because they will influence each other to behave in destructive lifestyles. The enemy will come to kill, steal, and destroy and foolish people will let the devil in.

I made a critical decision, and it paid off. I became so hungry for God and I wanted more of Him. God placed a burning desire within me for revival and miracles. I began to fast and pray, and God connected me with the right people. My spiritual leader travels all around the world preaching the gospel and God uses him to perform miracles. When I got connected to this man of God, a level of wisdom came to me along with impartation for miracles. My life and ministry shifted.

Dear Heavenly Father,

I thank you for your goodness and mercy. I humbly ask you to connect me to the right people that will cause my relationship with you to grow and deepen. Please remove the wrong people out of my life no matter how painful it may be. I don't want to be associated with foolishness but with righteousness. I decree that I will crucify this flesh, so I won't be tempted to hang out with a company of fools. Thank you for answering this prayer in Jesus' name. Amen.

DEVOTION FOURTEEN

Today's Scriptures For Meditation

Proverbs 14:1-2 says, "Every wise woman buildeth her house: but the foolish plucketh it down with her hands. He that walketh in his uprightness feareth the Lord: but he that is perverse in his ways despiseth him."

Have you ever heard the saying, "The grass is greener on the other side?" Well, many people have taken this saying to heart and realized that their current situation wasn't as bad as it seemed. The greener grass was just a mirage. A foolish person will complain about their blessings and take for granted those who God placed in their lives to cherish. A wise person will build up their home by finding ways to strengthen it for their family.

Years ago, I was that foolish woman that these scriptures mention. I literally tore down my own household while hurting those who cared about me in the process. I was bound by sin which caused me to be blind by my foolish actions. Once I repented and submitted my life to Christ, the blinders fell. I made a commitment to walk uprightly before God. As a result, God gave me a level of wisdom of ways that I can build my house instead of tearing it down.

Dear Heavenly Father,

I thank you for who you are. I repent for the times that I walked in ungratefulness and wasn't fully appreciative of life's blessings. I decree that I will fear you and follow all your commandments. Lord, I will walk uprightly before you and build up my home instead of tearing it down. I decree that I won't despise your ways. Thank you for answering this prayer in Jesus' name. Amen.

DEVOTION FIFTEEN

Today's Scripture For Meditation

Proverbs 14:29 Says, "He that is slow to wrath is of great understanding: but he that is hasty of spirit exalteth folly."

The Bible warns us many times about wrath and taking matters into our own hands. Many people lack patience, and they make assumptions without getting all the facts. This is a trick of the enemy. Before judging, we need to get a greater understanding because that's fair in God's sight. Don't take the bait of being hasty because it's a very foolish thing to do. Years ago, I was hasty when it came to anger.

I often testify about how God delivered me from anger. I was heading down a destructive path. I was violent and reacted without thinking about the consequences. One day, I destroyed someone's property because they had hurt and betrayed me. Shortly after, I was jailed and placed on probation for two years. I can reflect back and see how I had the spirit of folly. It wasn't until I repented and yielded my life unto God that I received deliverance. Over time, I was tested. People will smart talk me, and they can't even get a reaction out of me. The Lord has done a great work!

Dear Heavenly Father,

I exalt you and I humble myself. Many times, I exalted folly instead of you. I got outside of your will and wasn't a good representation of you. I made the wrong assumptions. I held on to grudges. I walked in offense. I even lashed out at people. I repent, and I forgive those who hurt me. I choose today to let all the frustration go. I want to walk in a manner that is pleasing in your sight. I love you Lord and I am grateful for your mercy.

DEVOTION SIXTEEN

Today's Scripture For Meditation

Proverbs 15:12 says, "A scorner loveth not one that reproveth him: neither will he go unto the wise.

A scorner or mocker in this scripture is someone who makes fun of wisdom. A scorner will not ask anyone for help. They can't handle healthy rebuke from a caring leader. They want to find out the hard way which is falling on their face. They fail to realize the help or the people that God sent in their lives to be a blessing to them somehow. They allow the enemy to deceive them by thinking that everyone is out to get them when it's the exact opposite.

A close friend of mines had many walls up. He had been disappointed by various failed relationships. Over time, he developed a mentality that said, "I trust no one except me." This mentality backfired on him. He lost his job and became ill. He couldn't afford the medication he needed. Many days went by and he had to humble himself. He was weak and realized that he had people in his life that genuinely cared about him. He told me what was going on and I rebuked him. I told him to never neglect himself again but ask for help. He agreed that he was wrong, and we got his medication. Remember to ask for help when you need it because it can cost you your life!

Dear Heavenly Father,

I humble myself. I don't want to have a hurt mentality and operate out of a wounded place. Bring me deliverance to my mind and my emotions. I don't want to despise the people you placed in my life to help me. I don't want to put walls up that shouldn't be there. Allow me to see the motives of people's heart towards me so I can be able to handle the correction. Thank you for answering this prayer in Jesus' name. Amen.

DEVOTION SEVENTEEN

Today's Scripture For Meditation

Proverbs 15:33 says, "The fear of the LORD is the instruction of wisdom; and before honour is humility."

Whenever we respect the Lord, we develop a reverence of Him in our lives. We don't want to grieve His spirit or do things that are contrary to His word. When we develop the fear of the Lord, we will notice that we will love things that He loves and hate the things that He hates. We will also develop discernment and be able to properly distinguish godly instructions versus carnal instructions. We tap into God's wisdom with Holy fear in our hearts; then God will honor us in many ways.

A major minister had to humble herself many years ago. She was a nobody when she first started her ministry meaning no one knew her name. No one would buy her books or cassette tapes. She knew she had a calling upon her life but often times she was frustrated because when she tried to promote herself, no doors were opening. One day, her pastor gave her a word from God and made her sit down for 3 years to receive instruction and training. She did it out of having a reverence for God. After that 3 years were up, God supernaturally launched her ministry, and she became a household name. Before honor is humility.

Dear Heavenly Father,

Bless me to have a holy fear in my heart so I can reverence you. I don't want to displease you, but I want my life and actions to glorify you. I want to receive your instructions whether you use a godly leader to give them to me or not. I decree that I will humble myself and whatever I do will be unto you and not man. You are righteous and just. I know that you will bring honor to my life in due season. Thank you for answering this prayer in Jesus' name. Amen.

DEVOTION EIGHTEEN

Today's Scripture For Meditation

Proverbs 16:16 says, "How much better is it to get wisdom than gold! and to get understanding rather to be chosen than silver!"

Silver and gold are considered valuable. However, God holds spiritual tools such as wisdom and understanding at a higher level. God has placed so much value on wisdom that His word says it's better to get wisdom than gold. The world may think this is foolish because they love money more than anything. People kill over money and do all kinds of terrible things to get more of it. If we placed the same value that God has on wisdom than He could show us many ways to get gold or money from multiple sources and the wisdom on how to keep it once we get it. It is better to get an understanding also than silver.

Many people's souls are perishing as they try to gain the world while dying spiritually in the process. They spend all their money on the latest trends and fashion but don't do anything for their spiritual life. They will spend hundreds of dollars on carnal things such as a secular concert, shoes, bags, electronics, etc. but refuse to pay tithes, invest in spiritual classes, books, or training. A world renown minister once said, "Wisdom is the how to." Can you imagine if you knew the "how to" to something then we would have fewer problems?

Dear Heavenly Father,

I repent of my sins. I love you so much. I want to value the things that you value. I realize how important spiritual things are and I decree that I will be a good steward over those things. I believe that you will cause me to prosper greatly if I apply these spiritual gifts. Lord, I pray that you will give me a greater understanding of wisdom and spiritual gifts. Thank you for answering this prayer in Jesus' name. Amen.

DEVOTION NINETEEN

Today's Scriptures For Meditation

Proverbs 17:27-28 says, "He that hath knowledge spareth his words: and a man of understanding is of an excellent spirit. Even a fool, when he holdeth his peace, is counted wise: and he that shutteth his lips is esteemed a man of understanding."

Wise people are associated with being coolheaded. They think things through and analyze the situation before speaking. They restrain from talking and hold back. However, on the other end, a foolish person just blurts things out that comes to their minds. They are hot-headed. These scriptures tell us that foolish people look wise if they can only keep their mouths shut. Have you ever seen someone who you thought was attractive until they opened their mouth and spoke? Foolish talk can make someone ugly. Once you get this understanding, then you will be of an excellent spirit.

Years ago, many people joked with me and called me a blonde because I had no filter. I literally spoke things out that made no sense. As the Lord began to strip things and people out of my life, I learned a very valuable lesson. This lesson was simple but necessary, "Think before you speak." Now, many people consider me a woman of wisdom because I don't react as I used too. I hold my tongue during a conflict, and I seek God before I release a prophetic word publicly.

Dear Heavenly Father,

I honor and adore you. Forgive me for all the times when I reacted foolishly in anger or spoke things that grieved your spirit. I love you so much. I truly need you to do a work in my life. Lord, do a mighty work in my life. Bless me not to be associated with foolishness. Bless me to think before I speak and keep a watch over my mouth. Lord, give me a greater level of wisdom so I can walk uprightly before you. Thank you for answering this prayer in Jesus' name. Amen.

DEVOTION TWENTY

Today's Scripture For Meditation

Proverbs 18:15 says, "The heart of the prudent getteth knowledge; and the ear of the wise seeketh knowledge."

A prudent person is an understanding person. This type of person gets knowledge or wants to go higher in life. For instance, they will put in the labor and work hard to find out everything they can in their career field, hobbies, and their calling. They will purchase books, webinars, magazines, or any material that will impart into them a greater depth of knowledge. They will also find themselves attracted to others that have the potential to take them to the next level or encourage them to become better than their current level. Therefore, the scripture says the ears of the wise seek knowledge.

When God first called me as a prophet, I had so many questions. I brought so many books on the prophetic and I studied them. I watched everything I could on YouTube on the prophetic ministry. The same thing happened when God was calling me to have a healing and deliverance ministry. I had no idea what deliverance was when I first heard of it. I had to do research and allow the Holy Spirit to highlight His word to me. I just couldn't get enough of studying these subject areas. My ears were seeking knowledge and yours should too!

Dear Heavenly Father,

I repent of my sins. I don't want to grieve you or hold back from seeking you. Lord, bless me to understand the things that you are calling me to do. Bless me to gain a greater depth of understanding of my career path. I decree that I am prudent and a God pleaser. Lord, bless my ears to seek knowledge. Allow me to find the right resource or person who will pour into me and equip me for greater. Thank you, Lord, for aligning my life in Jesus' name. Amen.

DEVOTION TWENTY ONE

Today's Scripture For Meditation

Proverbs 19:8 says, "He that getteth wisdom loveth his own soul: he that keepeth understanding shall find good."

How can you love your own soul? Why is getting wisdom beneficial? If you truly love yourself, then you are doing yourself a huge favor by getting wisdom on various topics or areas that you aren't knowledgeable of. You will take an interest in taking the necessary steps to strive despite the difficulties. This is one of the keys to success. Getting wisdom and putting the time and effort in. You can't fail, and you will find good like the scripture states.

For instances, when I started stepping out and teaching on the prophetic ministry, I started to attract a lot of warfare. The enemy was mad, and he sent witches to harm me. Witches would try to come into my room at night, get on my broadcasts, and come to my services. They would try to pray against me or distract the service. I had to gain wisdom. I find out how to pray against them according to scripture. I asked my leaders the experiences they had with witches. I did all of this because I love my soul and I will do anything to guard the anointing on my life.

Dear Heavenly Father,

I give you praise and Glory. I want to walk uprightly before you. I don't want to take things for granted and not apply myself. I decree that I will take the necessary steps to prepare myself for destiny and the things you are calling me to do. I decree that through you, I will be successful and will not fail. I can do all things through Christ that strengthens me. Thank you for answering this prayer in Jesus' name. Amen.

DEVOTION TWENTY TWO

Today's Scripture For Meditation

Proverbs 19:20 says, "Hear counsel, and receive instruction, that thou mayest be wise in thy latter end."

God places people in our lives that can help us become better or give us a better insight into something that we can't see. This is the benefit of having someone looking from the outside in. They can see things that you can't see, and their assessment can make a huge difference in our lives. We must realize that not everyone is out to get us or jealous of us. They might be genuine in their motives. If we can remain teachable and humble, then we can receive instructions. This is how we acquire wisdom in our latter days.

Years ago, when my husband first met me, I had about nine or ten book pages on Facebook. Each of my books had its own Facebook page. This means that every time I would write a book, I would create a new Facebook page for it. I became discouraged because I had a hard time getting people to like my new page. As I created a new page, the number of likes decreased. My husband kindly suggested that I delete those pages except for one and make the one page, an author page. I humbly obeyed and to my amazement, my page grew. The number of likes increased, and I was able to post all my book links, videos, and content on one page. My husband and I now look back on this and laugh. Thank God that I was able to receive instruction.

Dear Heavenly Father,

I humble myself, and I appreciate you bringing the right people to speak into my life. Lord, bless me to remain humble and teachable so I can be wise in my latter end. Lord, bless me to be able to discern who is giving me godly advice so I can grow and succeed in this life. I ask you to create in me a pure heart, so no pride or arrogance sets in. I decree that I will hear counsel, receive instruction, that I will be wise in my latter end. Thank you for answering this prayer in Jesus' name.

DEVOTION TWENTY THREE

Today's Scriptures For Meditation

Proverbs 22:17-19 says, "Bow down thine ear, and hear the words of the wise, and apply thine heart unto my knowledge. For it is a pleasant thing if thou keep them within thee; they shall withal be fitted in thy lips. That thy trust may be in the LORD, I have made known to thee this day, even to thee."

As you grow in wisdom, God will increase your sphere of influence and allow more people to hear your voice. In other words, more people will know who you are and will be able to hear your message. It is very important to pour into the right people and to listen to what wise people have to say. Many people are casting their pearls before the swine or wasting precious time and nuggets of wisdom on people who aren't interested. We need to incline our ears and apply what is being taught in our lives. We shouldn't take for granted the people that God places in our lives to pour into us. Often times God will connect people in our lives to help us in some measure on this journey such as getting ministering to after you poured out into others.

When I lived in Colorado Springs, my pastor always pushed me forward. I didn't want to fellowship with anyone but wanted to be alone. I had to get out of my comfort zone and learn how to be social. I planned a conference about prayer and not too many people came other than the church that I attended. My pastor sat me down many days later and told me that I had to advertise locally and become more sociable. At the time, it was difficult for me to hear but I received it. His valuable words stuck with me and I applied what he taught me to every event that I host.

Dear Heavenly Father,

I give you praise and honor. I decree that I trust you. I don't want to be in rebellion by not being subject to my leaders. I don't want to be high minded and full of pride. I want to be able to apply what I am taught by wise leaders. Lord, bless me to have a humble spirit. I rebuke the spirit of pride. I realize that you are pleased when I submit to those in authority. Thank you for answering this prayer in Jesus' name. Amen.

DEVOTION TWENTY FOUR

Today's Scriptures For Meditation

Proverbs 24:3-7 says, "Through wisdom is an house builded; and by understanding it is established: And by knowledge shall the chambers be filled with all precious and pleasant riches. A wise man is strong; yea, a man of knowledge increaseth strength. For by wise counsel thou shalt make thy war: and in multitude of counsellors there is safety. Wisdom is too high for a fool: he openeth not his mouth in the gate."

It takes wisdom to build a house or to manage a family. Just think about it, everyone must be on one accord in order to have a successful home. There needs to be rules set in place, so everyone knows what is to be expected. There must be curfews, chores, boundaries on what's allowed or what's not allowed. Everyone must understand what's to be expected for things to run smoothly. God can give us wisdom on how to run a household more efficiently.

In my home, we have rules set in place. On certain days, everyone has an assigned kitchen and bathroom duty. For example, my son's days to do the kitchen are on Tuesday and Thursday while my daughter's days are Monday and Wednesday. My children know that they must take showers in the morning before they go to school or they will not get their electronic devices. The reason is to make sure they smell fresh and clean throughout the school day. God gave us wisdom on how to instill this into our children because they went through a season of not wanting to take baths. Now, my children are trained, and they love to smell good. My husband and I had to impart wisdom into our children at a young age, so they can understand the importance of having rules and obeying them.

Dear Heavenly Father,

I give you glory! I repent of any disobedience and rebellion. Lord, bless my home to line up with your will. I decree that you will bring everything into alignment. I bind up any strife or confusion in the name of Jesus. Lord, bless my family to be in unity. Bless us to yield to your Spirit and any godly counsel that you placed in our lives. Lord, you tell us that a wise man is strong so bless us to be strong in you. Thank you for answering this prayer in Jesus' name. Amen.

DEVOTION TWENTY FIVE

Today's Scripture For Meditation

Proverbs 29:11 says, "A fool uttereth all his mind: but a wise man keepeth it in till afterwards."

Foolish people let nothing go pass them without expressing themselves. They don't hold back their emotions. A wise person is totally opposite.

God will give you wisdom on how to respond to a foolish person. He will give us words of wisdom and knowledge on how to respond. Sometimes God will put a guard over our mouths during times when we are provoked so we can remain silent. A wise person will not cast their pearls before the swine.

There was a lady who came to me to help her with her book. This was her first book, and she felt like she knew everything, and no one could tell her anything. She rejected any counsel that I was giving her. She even got out of character one day on the phone. I looked up to heaven and God intervened. I didn't get out of character and the phone disconnected. A few days later, this lady was very remorseful, and she apologized because she realized the many mistakes she had made during the publishing process. God gave me wisdom on how to respond during this stressful time when the enemy was trying to provoke me to get in my flesh.

Dear Heavenly Father,

Lord, I glorify you. I repent for the times I got out of character. I ask you to put a guard over my mouth and bless me to respond in the right way when the enemy is provoking me. I decree and declare that anger will not lodge within my bosom. I decree and declare that I will not get caught in foolish conversations. I decree and declare that I will be a wise person and that my actions will bring you Glory in Jesus' name. Amen.

DEVOTION TWENTY SIX

Today's Scripture For Meditation

Isaiah 55:9 says, "For as the heavens are higher than the earth, so are my ways higher than your ways, and my thoughts than your thoughts."

God has a major plan for our lives and many times we can't comprehend it. At times, God will speak things to us, and we must shift our way of thinking to embrace His plans. For instance, God may be calling you to launch an organization, but you may can't see how it will happen due to the lack of resources. The reality is that God doesn't need our money to make something happen, but He needs our faith. He can supernaturally provide the building, the funds, and the people to make it happen. God is fair, and He judges accordingly. He puts certain people into position and gives them a certain grace and authority.

God's ways are full of wisdom. God knew exactly what He was doing when He brought you through the transition. He knows how to rescue His people from trials. He knows how to chastise His children. Many times, when we suffer, we don't understand why. We tend to forget that God has a plan and He will get the glory out of it. God will work His miracles the way He chooses too. He will vindicate us how He feels is best. He will bless His children at the right moment. Remember, everything is working out for your good.

Dear Heavenly Father,

I exalt you. I know you have an amazing plan for my life. I choose to worship you and to walk uprightly before you. Instead of me complaining about the things that I don't have, I will praise you. Instead of me being lazy and nonproductive, I will be productive and labor in the Kingdom. Instead of me focusing on negativity, I will keep my focus on Jesus, so I can have perfect peace. I decree that I will trust you even when I don't understand what's going on. Thank you for answering this prayer in Jesus' name. Amen.

DEVOTION TWENTY SEVEN

Today's Scripture For Meditation

Daniel 2:23 says, "I thank thee, and praise thee, O thou God of my fathers, who hast given me wisdom and might, and hast made known unto me now what we desired of thee: for thou hast now made known unto us the king's matter."

Daniel was a powerful prophet who had the gift of dream interpretation. During a crisis in the kingdom, he didn't panic when faced with death. He remained calm because He trusted in God. When the King had a disturbing dream, he threatened to kill everyone in his court unless they could tell him what he dreamed and the meaning of it. Daniel did just that. After he sought God, he received wisdom and insight about the dream. No one died, and God received the glory.

God wants to give us wisdom about the spiritual gifts in our lives. He wants to give us strategies on when to use them and how to use them. He wants us to use these gifts to bring Him glory and to advance His kingdom. One of the strongest gifts on my life is the word of knowledge. Each time this gift is stirred up, God uses me in a different way than previously. God has given me wisdom on how to seek Him and how to flow in these gifts at the right time. He wants the same for you.

Dear Heavenly Father,

I give you praise and honor. Lord, I want wisdom on how to flow in the spiritual gifts you have placed in my life. Lord, if my gifts are lying dormant, I pray that you activate them. I decree that you will give me wisdom and insight to learn more about these gifts and the talents you have placed inside of me. Lord, bless me to be a good steward of these gifts and never use them for greed or selfish gain. I decree that the spiritual gifts on my life will bring you glory. Thank you for answering this prayer in Jesus' name. Amen.

DEVOTION TWENTY EIGHT

Today's Scripture For Meditation

Hosea 14:9 says, "Who is wise, and he shall understand these things? prudent, and he shall know them? for the ways of the Lord are right, and the just shall walk in them: but the transgressors shall fall therein."

Wise people know the ways of God and will walk in them. They don't want to grieve the Holy Spirit, and they are able to discern what's of God. However, the wicked stumble in the ways of God which causes their downfall. The wicked turned their back on the things of God and destruction hit their lives. God's ways are right, and God will give us wisdom, so we can understand it. People are perishing due to their ignorance. God wants to give us revelation, so we can know Him more.

Sadly, people fall and stumble all the time. I have seen leaders rise and fall. They started off right, but along the way, they allowed pride, lust, greed and other sins into their lives. They got distracted by the opportunities and the blessings. They forgot about God and they didn't seek Him for wisdom on how to handle the opportunities, the favor, and the popularity. The enemy wants us to stumble, but God can give us the wisdom to walk uprightly.

Dear Heavenly Father,

I give you glory. Bless me not to get distracted by the open doors and the blessings when it comes.

I want to keep my heart right and walk uprightly before you. Lord, I need to stay in prayer and stay connected to you. The flesh produces nothing righteous, and I want you to lead and guide me. Jesus, I decree that you are my source and I will keep my eyes upon you. Bless me with wisdom in every area of my life in Jesus' name. Amen.

DEVOTION TWENTY NINE

Today's Scripture For Meditation

Matthew 7:24 says, "Therefore whosoever heareth these sayings of mine, and doeth them, I will liken him unto a wise man, which built his house upon a rock:"

When we obey God and do what He tells us to do, then we are compared to a wise man building his foundation on the things of God. Building things on God is a sure and solid foundation which is compared to a rock. A rock will still be intact after a storm hits. However, some other elements such as sand or trees may shift during a storm. Therefore, building on the foundation of Jesus, who is the rock is wise. During the storm, Jesus will be our rock and our place of safety. After the storm, we will realize how much Jesus was a refuge to us during the storm.

When I was in my wilderness season, I found out that Jesus was my rock. When I was on probation, God gave me the strength to get through it. He is my refuge. People walked away from me and it hurt. I didn't understand why they left me, but God gave me wisdom. It had to happen to prepare me for my next season. God allowed me to see a glimpse of His plan for my life. Everything in my life that wasn't built on Him was shaken. God gave me wisdom through the storm and I quickly obeyed everything He put on my heart to do. I refused to prolong the wilderness season due to any disobedience or complaining.

Dear Heavenly Father,

I give you glory. I decree that I will be a doer of the word. I decree that I will be like the wise man in Matthew 7:24 that built his house upon a rock. I don't want to grieve you by doing things contrary to your will for my life. I refuse to complain during the tough times instead I will praise you. I decree that I will have an attitude of gratitude. Thank you for answering this prayer in Jesus' name. Amen.

DEVOTION THIRTY

Today's Scripture for Meditation

Luke 21:15 says, "For I will give you a mouth and wisdom, which all your adversaries shall not be able to gainsay nor resist."

On this journey, we will go through attacks. The enemy will send people to test us. This is what happened to Jesus. In Mark 12, the religious leaders tried to test him. They came to him and tried to puff him up by saying that he was a great teacher. However, Jesus was able to discern their true motives because he had the wisdom of God. Jesus was so wise that his enemies didn't have the right words to say. This made his enemies hate him even more. Jesus was able to speak the right words and none of his enemies could refute it.

Studying the word of God is key to the Christian life. We will cross paths with all kinds of people who have different belief systems. They won't always accept our moral beliefs, but God will give us wisdom. He will give us supernatural strategies to minister to others. He will fill our mouths with His words. He will give us words of knowledge, prophecy, and word of knowledge. The word of God coming out of our mouths will be so powerful that no one will be able to refute it.

Dear Heavenly Father,

I am grateful that you love to give your children wisdom. I don't always have the right words to say, but you do. I don't always know what to do, but you do. I know that when you guide my footsteps, I can't lose. I know that I have the victory in you. I know that you will protect me from my enemies. I know that if you sent me, then you will back me up. Thank you for answering this prayer in Jesus' name. Amen.

DEVOTION THIRTY ONE

Today's Scriptures For Meditation

Ephesians 5:15-16 says, "See then that ye walk circumspectly, not as fools, but as wise, Redeeming the time, because the days are evil."

The days we live in are extremely evil. There is a rise in school shootings, church shootings, and shootings in various places. There is also a rise of tragedies, terrorisms, homosexuality, and the list continues. In these evil days, many people are being led astray by false ministers. People are easily led astray when they aren't grounded in the word of God and don't test the spirit. It is wise to walk circumspectly or be very careful how we live.

In every generation, there is a rise of false ministers who called themselves "Jesus" or "The Second Elijah." They want to be worshiped. They want people to serve them. They lead people to themselves and not to God. The more you seek God, the more you will be able to recognize what's of Him and what's not of Him. I have witnessed people call false ministers "Jesus in the flesh" and change their last name to the last name of the false minister. It was very sickening to see. My prayers always go out to the people who are brained washed. Remember to walk circumspectly.

Dear Heavenly Father,

I magnify your name. I repent of all my sins. Lord, bless me to walk circumspectly. Bless me with an abundance of wisdom, so I will be able to discern who is of you or not. Bless me with the strength to resist temptation. I decree that I will crucify this flesh. Bless my family to walk uprightly before you. Lord, bless us with a hedge of protection in these evil days. Thank you for answering this prayer in Jesus' name. Amen.

DEVOTION THIRTY TWO

Today's Scriptures For Meditation

Colossians 2:2-3 says, "That their hearts might be comforted, being knit together in love, and unto all riches of the full assurance of understanding, to the acknowledgement of the mystery of God, and of the Father, and of Christ;

In whom are hid all the treasures of wisdom and knowledge."

Apostle Paul worked hard by laboring to make sure the Colossian church was in alignment with the will of God. He wrote a letter saying that even though some people of the Colossian church may have never seen him in person, he wanted them to be encouraged. He wanted to make sure they were unified together in love. He knew that this would lead to a greater understanding of Jesus and in Him is the hidden treasure of wisdom and knowledge.

I have made some mistakes along the way in ministry. I have lost focus of my purpose because of certain trials and distractions. I realize that ministry is an ever-learning call upon my life. When I focused on Jesus during the tough times, I was able to regain focus on my assignment. I recognize that I'm fulfilling my purpose all because of Him. Afterwards, a major shift happened in my life. I received a fresh outpouring of the anointing and began to see an influx of miracles.

Dear Heavenly Father,

I exalt your Holy name. Bless me to walk in unity with other believers and not division. Bless me to walk in love and show others your love who may not know it. Bless me to come into a greater understanding of the mystery of the kingdom and the Godhead. I recognize that the fear of the Lord is the beginning of all knowledge. I decree that I will press into you and not quit when things get hard. Thank you for answering this prayer in Jesus' name. Amen.

DEVOTION THIRTY THREE

Today's Scripture For Meditation

Colossians 3:16 says, "Let the word of Christ dwell in you richly in all wisdom; teaching and admonishing one another in psalms and hymns and spiritual songs, singing with grace in your hearts to the Lord."

Believers are called to encourage each other with the spiritual wisdom they received. This starts by letting the word of God live inside of their hearts and minds. How can the word of God dwell in us? The answer is by meditation. We must reflect on the word and digest the word. When we do this, then we give the Holy Spirit something to work with. The word will flow out of us as a rushing river. We will be amazed at how much God will use us to pour into others in various ways such as psalms, hymns, spiritual songs, singing, teaching, prophesying, and more.

Every day people come to me with all kinds of problems. I may not know the answer, but God does. I quickly pray and get back to the person. It amazes me how a passage that I recently read out of the bible comes back to my remembrance. I am able to provide godly counsel without giving them carnal advice. The times I took to meditate on the word of God paid off. The word flowed out of my mouth in the time of need. Take time to get the word of God deep within your heart daily so God can use you in a powerful way.

Dear Heavenly Father,

I give you praise. Lord, bless me to be able to give godly counsel instead of carnal advice. I know that you are the ultimate problem solver. I know that with the same comfort I received from you that I am able to comfort someone else. I decree that I will die to self so that I can do great exploits for your kingdom. I decree that I will walk in a spirit of excellence. Thank you for answering this prayer in Jesus' name. Amen.

DEVOTION THIRTY FOUR

Today's Scriptures For Meditation

Colossians 4:5-6 says, "Walk in wisdom toward them that are without, redeeming the time. Let your speech be always with grace, seasoned with salt, that ye may know how ye ought to answer every man."

The word of God tells us to be wise when we are around unbelievers. We must be careful in the way we act and the words we speak. They are watching our lives, and we are meant to be set apart. They are looking for a good reason to serve the God that we serve. They may want to know why we serve God. Therefore, the bible warns us to be careful around them because one day they may be believers. We must remember that we represent Jesus Christ on this earth.

When I was in the word, I was afraid of Christians. I knew they were different because of how they dressed and the life that they lived. When I was going to clubs, they were in bible study. My younger sister got saved, and my childhood home was full of Christians doing a bible study every week. I can honestly say they were great ambassadors of Christ and walked in wisdom. I never saw them lose their temper instead I saw them as being blessed and full of joy. I couldn't understand why they were so happy. They made me feel loved and accepted when I came around them. Their wisdom on how to minister to the lost won me over to the kingdom of God.

Dear Heavenly Father,

Bless me to walk in wisdom around unbelievers. Bless them to feel your love and presence coming off me. Bless the unbelievers that I encounter to want to know you. Bless me with strategies to witness to the lost. I decree that I will walk in wisdom and a spirit of excellence. I decree that my speech will be seasoned with salt and that I will know how to answer every man accordingly. Thank you for answering this prayer in Jesus' name. Amen.

DEVOTION THIRTY FIVE

Today's Scripture For Meditation

1 Corinthians 1:25 says, "Because the foolishness of God is wiser than men; and the weakness of God is stronger than men."

The world couldn't understand the messages of the gospel. The wisest of the world's scholars couldn't understand it. The world feels like the wisdom of God is foolish, but it works and saves the lost. Their intellectual mind can't comprehend the life, burial, and resurrection of Jesus. God's wisdom is so strong that He is able to bring conversion to people's lives. The wise people of the world who experienced conversion are now on fire for God. God uses the foolish things to confound the wise.

Once the gospel was foolish to me. I thought all Christians were crazy. I didn't understand why Christians didn't do the sinful things that I was doing at the time. Sinning was fun to me but once I heard the gospel of Jesus my eyes opened. I saw how the enemy had me bound. God called me and gave me an opportunity to receive salvation. He chose me to preach His gospel. Yes, the same message that I once thought was foolish. God chooses who He wants to choose. Many are called, but few are chosen.

Dear Heavenly Father,

I give you all the honor and glory. I humble myself. Bless me to never forget where I came from. If there is any wicked thing in my heart, please remove it now. You use the foolish things to confound the wise. You use the weak things of the world to confound the mighty. Bless my mind to be open to receive the things that you are showing me. You warn me in the word that a natural mind can't discern the things of God. Bless me to not miss out on the opportunities that you have for me. Thank you for answering this prayer in Jesus' name. Amen.

DEVOTION THIRTY SIX

Today's Scripture For Meditation

James 1:5 says, "If any of you lack wisdom, let him ask of God, that giveth to all men liberally, and upbraideth not; and it shall be given him."

All throughout this book, we have repeatedly seen how God loves to give us wisdom. We truly need it. Many people are called to do amazing things in this earth, but they need the wisdom of God to ensure their success. All kinds of challenges may arise however the wisdom of God will combat these issues. New doors and opportunities will open, and the wisdom of God will help us to have achievement. There will be many people who will try to take over the vision that God gave us, but with God's wisdom, we will overcome.

In ministry, new challenges arise often, and I have no idea on what to do. However, God does. I will go to pray and fast until I get a plan from heaven on what to do. Without the counsel of God, I would've faced a significant loss, warfare, and much worse. For instance, once someone tried to take over my business. This person wanted to take my business in another direction from which God was leading me. God gave me wisdom which was to expose the spirit behind the attack and disconnect from the source. Without the wisdom of God, I would've still been connected to the foolishness I was enduring.

Dear Heavenly Father,

I exalt your name. I give you praise. I am truly grateful that you love to give your people wisdom without any rebukes. You don't think of us less for asking for it. You want your people to ask for it, so you can bring us a major deliverance in various areas of our lives. You are righteous and just. For every problem that I face you already have the solution. Bless me to press into your presence, so I can always gain clarity and direction. Thank you for answering this prayer in Jesus' name. Amen.

DEVOTION THIRTY SEVEN

Today's Scripture For Meditation

James 3:13 says, "Who is a wise man and endued with knowledge among you? let him shew out of a good conversation his works with meekness of wisdom."

True wisdom is shown by the way we live our lives on this earth. People can see us walking in wisdom when we are humble and by doing great works that glorify God. We don't have to try to impress people by dropping names of famous people we may know or boasting on ourselves. Just produce the fruit or the evidence of what you are called to do. God will bring recognition and put you in demand. God will back you up and prove Himself to be true through you. It's better to let other people boast on you than yourself. Continue doing great works so God can be glorified.

I meet many leaders in the body of Christ. They weren't impressed by my looks, the works that I produced, or who I was connected to. They were impressed by my character. They said that I was meek and approachable. Some of these leaders promoted me by sharing my flyers or statuses on social media. They even told other people to connect with me. When we had a conversation, I let them do most of the talking because I wanted to sit at their feet and learn. Be humble, stay teachable, and let your fruits speak for itself. God will open the right doors at the right time with the right people.

Dear Heavenly Father,

I give you glory. I repent for the times that I allowed pride to get in my heart. Bless me to remain teachable and not overly promote myself or business. I decree that I will allow you to promote me because when you do it the doors just swing opens. I decree that I will go through the necessary process, so you can prune me and bring out the right fruits and attributes within me. I decree that everything I do will bring glory to your name. Thank you for answering this prayer in Jesus' name. Amen.

DEVOTION THIRTY EIGHT

Today's Scripture For Meditation

James 3:17 says, "But the wisdom that is from above is first pure, then peaceable, gentle, and easy to be intreated, full of mercy and good fruits, without partiality, and without hypocrisy."

The wisdom that God gives us is pure. There is no contamination or impurities that come with it. God's wisdom comes with no strings attached. God's wisdom will give you peace because there is a surety that you are making the right decisions. God's wisdom is gentle because He is very patience. God's wisdom is easy to please and we will be satisfied with the results. The wisdom God gives us will be a blessing to others. The wisdom that God gives is fair and honest.

God gave Joseph wisdom to provide a strategy for the upcoming famine (Genesis 41:25-57). The wisdom that God gave Joseph lead to his promotion to 2nd in command in Egypt. Many people have come to me for counsel and God gave me wisdom on how to counsel them accordingly. Their minds were open, and they were transformed after they received what the Lord gave me to release. When you seek God and obey Him, He will give you a level of wisdom to impact the lives of others.

Dear Heavenly Father,

I humble myself in your presence. I am grateful that you generously give me wisdom that will be a blessing to others. I am grateful that your wisdom is pure, peaceable, gentle, easy to be intreated, full of mercy and good fruits, without partiality, and without hypocrisy. Lord, give me the spirit of wisdom so that I can be used by you to impart this spirit into the lives of others. Thank you for answering this prayer in Jesus' name. Amen.

DEVOTION THIRTY NINE

Today's Scripture For Meditation

Psalm 19:7 says, "The law of the Lord is perfect, converting the soul: the testimony of the Lord is sure, making wise the simple."

The word of God is pure, just, and Holy. His word, laws, and instructions are for our good.

The word of God gives us the strength to continue the good fight of faith. When we feel like giving up, the word of God provides us strength. The word is able to revive the dead places in our lives. The testimonies of the Lord can be tested. God provides testimonies, so we can stay encouraged. When we apply the word of God to our lives, it will make us wise.

Many people are amazed that I am knowledgeable about certain topics at such a young age. I give the credit to the Lord because He blessed me to gain a level of understanding. The wisdom that I obtained from the Lord came from prayer, fasting, studying the word, and devotion. God is no respecter of a person. God longs to make you wise in every area of your life. He wants all His children to live a blessed, prosperous, and purposeful life.

Dear Heavenly Father,

Thank you so much for sending your son Jesus to die for my sins. He is the ultimate example of my faith. He is the reason that I am able to seek you and have a deeper relationship with you.

Thank you for giving me your word as an example to follow. Your word provides wisdom, training, rebuke, and instruction in righteousness. When I apply your word to my life, I gain tools to equip me for every task set before me. Thank you for answering this prayer in Jesus' name. Amen.

DEVOTION FORTY

Today's Scripture For Meditation

Hosea 4:6 says, "My people are destroyed for lack of knowledge: because thou hast rejected knowledge, I will also reject thee, that thou shalt be no priest to me: seeing thou hast forgotten the law of thy God, I will also forget thy children."

Many people are being led astray in these last evil and wicked days. They have no discernment and can't tell the difference between good and evil. They don't want to hear the truth of the gospel. They would rather hear a message that will tickle their ears. People are destroyed because they have no knowledge about the things of God. If they reject the knowledge of God, then God will reject them. When God rejects us, that's a scary thing because there's no hope or chance of redemption.

Many years ago, I had no knowledge about finances, faith, the gifts of the spirit, and the list continues. I was living a dry, unfruitful life. Even though I was in church, I was on the path of destruction because I rejected the things of God due to a lack of understanding. At the time, I wasn't a student of the word and I was a friend of the world. It took a trial for me to stop compromising and to get on fire for God. From this day forth, I find out as much as I can find out about a topic, so I can increase in learning.

Dear Heavenly Father,

Open my eyes so I can see the things that you want me to see. Bless me to stay in your will and not get off track. Lord, set me on fire for you and deepen my passion for you. Bless me to do my research on an area that you are calling me too. Allow me to be a good steward over the gifts and talents that you have placed inside of me. Thank you for answering this prayer in Jesus' name. Amen.

DEVOTION FORTY ONE

Today's Scripture For Meditation

Isaiah 33:6 says, "And wisdom and knowledge shall be the stability of thy times, and strength of salvation: the fear of the Lord is his treasure."

Everyone goes through trials in life. We go through good seasons then bad seasons. Yet, the

Lord will give us stability in the rocky times just like He did Elijah when he was by the brook (1 Kings 17). God will provide wisdom and knowledge to get us through the dark times. God will provide supernatural strength of His love, joy, peace, and comfort during the tribulations. God will provide an abundance of wisdom during these times. When we look to Him, we can find the treasuries of the deeper things of Him.

When I was in the wilderness season, everything in my life was drying up. I could no longer do certain things that I was used too. For instance, instead of paying $90 a month for satellite tv. God bless me with wisdom to get Netflix for around $12 a month. Instead of eating out every week, God gave me the wisdom to cook more meals at home and buy generic brand products. During this transitional season, I pressed more into God and I received peace. I knew deep down that everything will be okay. I know that in the kingdom, the way up is down. Eventually, God started to restore my life. If God brought me through it, then He can do it for you.

Dear Heavenly Father,

I give you praise God. You are awesome. I thank you for sustaining me in the tough times. I thank you for providing a ram in the bush. I decree that I am an overcomer. I decree that I am more than a conqueror through Christ Jesus. I decree that I will walk in victory everywhere I go. I decree that all my needs will be met and that my feet will be secure. I decree that I am coming out of the dry places into a land of prosperity. Thank you for answering this prayer in Jesus' name. Amen.

DEVOTION FORTY TWO

Today's Scripture For Meditation

2 Chronicles 1:10 says, "Give me now wisdom and knowledge, that I may go out and come in before this people: for who can judge this thy people, that is so great?"

This was Solomon's prayer. He never asked for riches or fame. Instead, he asked for wisdom, so he could guide the people in the right direction. Since he didn't ask for wealth, God bless him with wealth anyways. Solomon recognized the importance of asking for wisdom because he knew that he couldn't lead people effectively without the help of God. When we rely on God, it will keep us humble. Many people do things in their own strength and end up getting frustrated and quitting their assignment. When we have the wisdom of God, then we receive supernatural strength to finish any task.

Oftentimes I felt inadequate and unqualified to stand in the presence of God's people. I knew that there are people out there who were better speakers, preachers, authors, singers, etc. than me. I knew that only God can give me the right words and messages to speak to His people. Before I minister, I seek God for the messages I am to speak or how He wants the service to go. I believe this is one of the reasons why there are many healings, word of knowledge, prophecies, etc. because I press into Him and allow Him to flow. Remember to seek God on what He wants to do in every area of your life.

Dear Heavenly Father,

I give you praise. Lord, give me wisdom on how to lead your people. Bless me with the right words to speak. Bless me with the right counsel to provide to people when they come and ask me for advice. Bless me to help guide people and point them back to you always. Bless me to be sensitive to your presence, so I can flow with you. Lord, bless me to live a supernatural life. Thank you so much for answering this prayer in Jesus' name. Amen.

DEVOTION FORTY THREE

Today's Scriptures For Meditation

Romans 11:33-34 says, "O the depth of the riches both of the wisdom and knowledge of God! how unsearchable are his judgments, and his ways past finding out! For who hath known the mind of the Lord? or who hath been his counsellor?"

Just when we discover something new in God, we find out that there is more. There is a deeper level and realm of God. We can go as high in God as we want to go. Many people are just satisfied with going to church and hearing a good word and going home afterwards. They never apply what was taught in their lives. It's time for us to press into God and enter the depths of knowledge that He has. God is multifaceted and there are many levels to Him that we have yet to tap into.

Who can understand the ways of God? When God called me as a prophet, I quickly discover there are many dimensions to being a prophet. For instance, different functions, anointings, characteristics, flows, etc. Some people just think that prophets go around prophesying all day and night. Not true! I discovered that prophets are called to pray, guide, directive, rebuke, encourage, comfort, intercede, bring the presence of God to certain regions, and the list continues. As I was faithful over a certain measure of grace of the prophetic anointing, God would increase the gifting on my life. I can't be satisfied with how God used me in the past. I want to go higher because I know there is more. Always strive to grow! Never get complacent in your gift.

Dear Heavenly Father,

I give you glory. Thank you for being so faithful. I am grateful that there are depths of knowledge and wisdom to you. I am thankful that you are just, and you lead and guide me. Lord, give me a burden for prayer and intercession. Lord, bless my thoughts to be pleasing in your sight. I come against anything that will grieve you. I decree that I will not neglect you but be sensitive to your presence. Thank you for answering my prayer in Jesus' name. Amen.

DEVOTION FORTY FOUR

Today's Scripture for Meditation

Proverbs 3:7 says, "Be not wise in thine own eyes: fear the Lord, and depart from evil."

Don't be wise in your own eyes because we are imperfect people. People are going to make mistakes in life. Many people felt like they knew what they were doing and rejected help and over time they stumble because pride set in. Pride comes before destruction. Pride is an abomination before the Lord. We are called to respect the Lord and live right. When we respect the Lord, there is a dependency on Him. This will cause us to walk in humility and not depend on our own strength. Also, God will give us the strength to shun evil.

A powerful man of God that I know once struggled with pride for a season. God used him mightily in my life to break strongholds off me. I am forever grateful, but no matter how anointed you are you can still stumble due to pride. This is what happened to this man of God. He was hurt by someone and it manifested in all his preaching. He hurt and embarrassed the person who hurt him publicly. One day God woke me up at 2 am and I seen this man of God in a vision. On his forehead was Proverbs 3:7. It was disturbing to see, but I couldn't shake it, so I knew I had to tell him what I saw. I inboxed his wife and him on social media. They rebuked me, but later the man of God approached me. He confirmed that the dream was right, and he needed to hear it. He later reconciled with the person who hurt him.

God will use people in different ways to get His message across.

Dear Heavenly Father,

I repent of my sins. I glorify you. Bless me not to get caught up in gifts but allow me to focus on my character. I want to have great characteristics of Jesus Christ. I love you so much and I don't want to grieve the Holy Spirit. I decree that I won't be wise in my own eyes! I decree that I will fear the Lord and depart from evil all the days of my life. I decree that I will walk in humility. I decree that I will be open to receive a rebuke from someone that you sent to keep me in your will. I give you any burdens that I am carrying. Thank you for answering this prayer in Jesus' name. Amen.

DEVOTION FORTY FIVE

Today's Scripture For Meditation

Proverbs 26:12 says, "Seest thou a man wise in his own conceit? there is more hope of a fool than of him."

The bible says there is more hope for a foolish person than someone who thinks they are wise in their own eyes. This doesn't mean not to think of yourself as smart, but this means a prideful person who has an unteachable spirit. This type of person will consider themselves a one-stop shop and reject the help of others. This is another reason this scripture states that there is more hope for a fool than of him. A fool may be more open to receiving correction than a prideful man. No one person has everything. There are many members in the body of Christ, but there is one body. Therefore we need each other. Prophets need other prophets, teachers need other teachers, etc.

There is a pastor who has a deliverance ministry. He travels the world preaching the gospel and casting out devils. However, he comes off as arrogant. He spoke a lot of things out of his mouth that he later had to repent for publicly. He felt like he knew everything until one day he met his match in the spirit. This pastor said, "Deliverance ministers don't need security." One day, 3 demon-possessed men got up in the middle of his preaching. They began to curse and rush at him while he was behind the pulpit. One of the men tackled the pastor down to the floor. Some people in the pews ran and helped the pastor.

They worked together to pin these demonized men down to the floor. The demons in these men gave them extraordinary strength. Some demons were eventually cast out after a wrestling match. The pastor had his staff call the police, and he confessed the importance of having security. He was shaken up after this ordeal.

Dear Heavenly Father,

I give you praise and glory. I decree that I will remain humble and teachable. Bless me to not speak on things that I am not knowledgeable of. I decree and declare that I will not reject your help. I will not be wise in my own eyes. Lord, bless me to trust you and press into you more. Lord, increase my zeal and hunger for you. I decree that I will meditate on your word day and night. I decree that I will walk in the spirit, so I will not fulfill the lusts of the flesh. Thank you for answering this prayer in Jesus' name. Amen.

DEVOTION FORTY SIX

Today's Scripture For Meditation

Isaiah 5:21 says, "Woe unto them that are wise in their own eyes, and prudent in their own sight!"

A woe is a warning. It is a terrible thing to be wise in our own eyes. We have previously covered why but let's look at some other scriptures that confirm this warning. Jeremiah 9:23 warns us about boasting. We are warned about boasting in wisdom, strength, and finances in this scripture. We should be boasting about the goodness of the Lord because He is eternal and everything else is temporary. When we die, we can't take the car, money, clothes, house, etc. with us. We can have something one day and lose it the next day. Things happen such as natural disasters, sickness, loss of relationships, etc. that will cause a major loss in people's lives. For instance, in 2010, I owned a house. In 2014, I lost it, yet God is slowly restoring the things I've lost.

There was a beautiful fashion design blogger. She was wealthy, young, and she could have anything that she wanted. She had so many handbags, shoes, perfumes, and the list continues. One day she got sick and found out that she had cancer. She was dying, and she realized that she couldn't take any of her belongings with her. I'm not sure what her relationship with God was, but it was a sad story. She wrote her last blog and passed away shortly after. To paraphrase she wrote something like this, "I could buy anything that I want, but life is more than money and fashion." Her last words went viral over the internet. We need God's strength and His wisdom. We need to boast about what He has done in our lives and His promises. Heaven and earth will pass away but His words will remain (Matthew 24:35).

Dear Heavenly Father,

I give you glory and praise! Thank you for warning me. You chastise those who you love. You love me so much that you gave me your word. I pray that my heart is not hard. I decree that your word will fall on good ground. I decree that I will not get caught up in idolizing carnal temporal things. I decree that I will focus on Jesus, so I can do what I am called to do. Bless me to discover my purpose and my next assignment. Thank you for answering this prayer in Jesus' name. Amen.

DEVOTION FORTY SEVEN

Today's Scripture For Meditation

Proverbs 21:30 says, "There is no wisdom nor understanding nor counsel against the Lord."

There is no wisdom, counsel, or advice that can stand or succeed against the Lord. A fool will come against the Lord. A fool says in his heart that there is no God (Psalm 14:1). The counsel of the Lord will stand (Proverbs 19:21). It doesn't matter who doesn't like it or agree with it. It is a dangerous thing to go against God. Many people have perished because they tried to fight God. Pharaoh was stubborn in the book of Exodus. He refused to let the people of God go. He perished in the Red Sea. The Sons of Korah went against the will of God and God opened the earth and swallowed them (Numbers 16:32).

When I did my second "Empowering the New Me" Conference, a witch came to disturb the service. She tried to blend in with everyone and hide in the crowds. My family and some people that were ministering felt that something wasn't right about her. I had a check in my spirit immediately when I first saw her walked into the room. When I was praying corporately, she was praying something else. She couldn't match the power of God that was flowing. God didn't want me to get distracted by her but to focus on Him. He performed many signs, wonders, and miracles that night. I later heard that the witch faced some repercussions for trying to come against the move of God.

Remember, there is no wisdom, understanding, or counsel against God.

Dear Heavenly Father,

I exalt you. I glorify you. I am thankful for your protection in my life. I decree that I will stay underneath your will because it's the safest place to be. Bless me with discernment so I can know what is in your will for my life. Bless me to never go against you. Bless me with an abundance of knowledge, wisdom, and understanding. Bless me to be a great steward over what you have given me and what you will give me. Thank you for answering this prayer in Jesus' name. Amen.

DEVOTION FORTY EIGHT

Today's Scriptures For Meditation

1 Corinthians 2:6-8 says, "Howbeit we speak wisdom among them that are perfect: yet not the wisdom of this world, nor of the princes of this world, that come to nought: But we speak the wisdom of God in a mystery, even the hidden

wisdom, which God ordained before the world unto our glory: Which none of the princes of this world knew: for had they known it, they would not have crucified the Lord of glory."

Have you ever seen someone who could articulate the scriptures in a profound way? It's like they are a walking bible and can quote any verse out of the word of God. God equips His people with the wisdom that doesn't come from this world. His wisdom is like a mystery, and the more we seek Him the more it's revealed. Many people in the world don't understand it. They feel like this wisdom is based on certain factors such as having an education or being old. Yet, God can supernaturally download information in our spirit and we will just know things. If people in Jesus' day were really wise, then they would've never crucified Him.

Many people have told me that I was very wise to be so young. They don't fully understand that everything that I teach is imparted to me by the Holy Spirit. Spiritual maturity isn't based on age. God gave me the revelation about many topics such as righteousness, faith, miracles, wisdom, etc. through the encounters I had with His presence. These encounters lead to me writing books. I was just hungry for Him and I obeyed what He told me to do. God can give you wisdom beyond your natural years as well. Obey Him and be a good steward over what He gives to you.

Dear Heavenly Father,

I give you glory. You are worthy to be praised. Bless me with the wisdom beyond my natural years so I can lead your people effectively and give the right counsel. Bless me to be equipped to do mighty exploits in the earth. Lord, sharpen the spiritual gifts within me so people can give you glory when I minister to them. Lord, give me the revelation of the mysteries of the kingdom. Thank you for answering this prayer in Jesus' name. Amen.

DEVOTION FORTY NINE

Today's Scripture For Meditation

1 Corinthians 2:14 says, "But the natural man receiveth not the things of the Spirit of God: for they are foolishness unto him: neither can he know them, because they are spiritually discerned."

A person who does not have the spirit of God can't understand the things that come from the spirit of God. They will consider things of the spirit foolish but only the spirit of God within a person can determine things to be true. A person without the spirit of God will probably reject the things of God. For instance, a person who is bound by carnality probably won't believe that people hear God or that He does miraculous things. However, a person with the spirit of God within them will believe that God does speak and believe in His miracles.

There is a popular show on television where a group of celebrity women gather around a table, drink coffee, and discuss current issues. One of these women mocked Vice President Pence because He said He hears from God. She said that He was crazy. Her mind couldn't comprehend how real God is and that He still speaks. Her words were all over the news and social media. Shortly after this, she was fired from her position on the television show. The world thinks it is crazy when people say, "I hear God." They will try to medicate the person or put them in a mental institution. A natural man can't comprehend the things of the Spirit of God.

Dear Heavenly Father,

I exalt you. You warn us in the word that a carnal mind is hostile to you. I know that when my thoughts are an enmity towards you, then I am not pleasing you. I decree that I will renew my mind, so I will not be conformed to this world. Bless me to be more sensitive to your presence, so I can know what's in your will. Bless me to not miss out on what you are doing. I rebuke any doubt, double-mindedness, fear, and unbelief in the name of Jesus. I decree that I have the mind of Christ on today in Jesus' name. Amen.

About The Author

Kimberly Moses started off her ministry as Kimberly Hargraves. She is highly sought after as a prophetic voice, intercessor and prolific author. There is no doubt that she has a global mandate on her life to serve the nations of the world by spreading the Gospel of Jesus Christ. She has a quickly expanding worldwide healing and deliverance ministry. Kimberly Moses wears many hats to fulfill the call God has placed on her life as an entrepreneur over several businesses including her own personal brand Rejoice Essentials which promotes the Gospel of Jesus Christ.

She also serves as a life coach and mentor tomany women. She is also the loving mother of two wonderful children. She is married to Tron. Kimberly has dedicated her life to the work of ministry and to serve others under the call God has placed over her life. Kimberly currently resides inSouth Carolina.

She is a very anointed woman of God who signs, miracles and wonders follow. The miraculous and incessant testimonies attributed to her ministry are incalculable, with many reporting physical and mental healing, financial breakthroughs, debt cancellations and other favorable outcomes. She is known across the globe as a servant who truly labors on behalf of God's people through intercession.

She is the author of The Following:

"Overcoming Difficult Life Experiences with Scriptures and Prayers"
"Overcoming Emotions with Prayers"
"Daily Prayers That Bring Changes"
"In Right Standing,"
"Obedience Is Key,"
"Prayers That Break The Yoke Of The Enemy: A Book Of Declarations,"
"Prayers That Demolish Demonic Strongholds: A Book Of Declarations,"
"Work Smarter. Not Harder. A Book Of Declarations For The Workforce,"
"Set The Captives Free: A Book Of Deliverance."
"Pray More Challenge"

"Walk By Faith: A Daily Devotional"
"Empowering The New Me: Fifty Tips To Becoming A Godly Woman"
"School of the Prophets: A Curriculum For Success"
"8 Keys To Accessing The Supernatural"
"Conquering The Mind: A Daily Devotional"
"Enhancing The Prophetic In You"
"The ABCs of The Prophetic: Prophetic Characteristics"

You can find more about Kimberly at
www.kimberlyhargraves.com

Reference

1. "Wisdom." Merriam-Webster.com. Accessed November 17, 2018. https://www.merriam-webster.com/dictionary/wisdom.

Index

A
abomination, 152
abundance, 5, 11, 162
adversaries, 109
anger, 3–4, 65, 78, 96
anointing, 21, 29, 32, 83, 116, 149
anxiety, 13–14

B
benefits, 6, 15, 17, 86
bitter, 4, 57
blessings, 35, 39, 62, 68, 104, 134–35

C
carnal mind, 21, 168
comfort, 120, 143, 149
commandments, 63
confidence, 7, 16–17
conversion, 125

counsel, 23–24, 29, 38, 52–53, 87, 128, 134, 160, 162

D
decree, 18–21, 54, 63, 84, 96, 102, 108, 120, 123, 132, 144, 153, 156, 159, 168
deliverance, 14, 65, 69, 80, 129, 170
depths, 23, 80–81, 149–50
discern, 2, 24, 41, 56, 87, 110, 114, 126
dreams, 11, 13–14, 26, 101, 152

E
enemy, 7, 13–14, 24, 41, 59, 65, 68, 83, 95–96, 104, 109–11, 125, 170

F
faith, 98, 137, 140, 164, 171
forgive, 26, 54, 57, 66, 78
freedom, 10, 12
fruits, 5, 12, 131, 133, 135

G
gifts, 2, 5–6, 21, 101–2, 140–41, 153
godly counsel, 54, 57, 119–20

H

health, 9–10

heart, 4–5, 20–21, 25–26, 29–30, 33, 36, 48, 50–51, 53, 56–57, 71–72, 105, 107, 118–19, 159–60

homosexuality, 113

honor, 11, 38–39, 42, 71–72, 78, 90, 102, 125

humiliation, 32

humility, 70–71, 152–53

hypocrisy, 12, 133, 135

I

instructions, 7, 20, 23, 31, 36, 45, 70, 72, 85–87, 136, 138

intercession, 150, 170

J

Jesus, 21, 32, 47, 93, 99, 105, 107, 110, 113, 116, 125, 159, 168

K

kingdom, 21, 50, 99, 101, 117, 120, 122, 143, 165

knowledge, 19, 32, 36, 54, 79–81, 88, 101, 110, 116–17, 130, 140, 145–46, 149–50, 162

L

leaders, 29, 32, 44, 83, 90, 104, 131

M

marriage, 3, 53
medication, 68
ministry, 16, 59, 71, 116, 128, 169–70
miracles, 17, 59, 98, 116, 161, 164, 167, 170
miraculous, 167, 170
money, 3, 47, 74, 98, 158–59
motives, 41, 53, 69, 86, 110
mysteries, 21, 115, 117, 163–65

P

patience, 65, 134
peace, 7, 11–12, 39, 44, 134, 143
praise, 83, 90, 99, 102, 108, 120, 129, 147, 156
prayer, 17–18, 24, 30, 33, 39, 42, 44, 87, 89–90, 111, 113–14, 135, 137–38, 150, 170
promises, 9, 15, 38–39, 159
promotion, 15–16, 41, 134
prophets, 13, 80, 101, 149, 155, 171
prosperity, 11, 144
protection, 6–7, 35, 114, 162

R

rebellion, 42, 90, 93
refuge, 107
repent, 24, 26, 32, 42, 48, 50–51, 54, 57, 62, 66, 75, 81, 96, 153, 155
riches, 11, 13, 38–39, 115, 146

S
strength, 4, 107, 114, 137, 142, 146, 152, 158–59
supernatural, 35, 171

T
trials, 98, 116, 140, 142
troublemakers, 41
truth, 29, 35, 140

U
understanding, 19, 22–23, 36, 38–39, 48, 65, 74–77, 81, 91, 115–17, 137, 140, 162
ungratefulness, 62

V
value, 74–75
victory, 111, 144

W

warfare, 83, 128

wisdom, 1–6, 8–19, 23, 35–36, 38–41, 49–51, 74–75, 82–83, 100–102, 104–5, 121–23, 127–31, 134–35, 158–60, 162–65

www.ingramcontent.com/pod-product-compliance
Lightning Source LLC
Chambersburg PA
CBHW052131110526
44591CB00012B/1680